stampwork

stampwork

Creative decorating ideas for the home

Sacha Cohen
Photography by Lizzie Orme

southwater

This edition is published by Southwater

Southwater is an imprint of
Anness Publishing Limited
Hermes House
88–89 Blackfriars Road
London SE1 8HA
tel. 020 7401 2077
fax 020 7633 9499

Distributed in the UK by
The Manning Partnership
251–253 London Road East
Batheaston
Bath BA1 7RL
tel. 01225 852 727
fax 01225 852 852

Distributed in the USA by
Anness Publishing Inc.
27 West 20th Street
Suite 504
New York
NY 10011
tel. 212 807 6739
fax 212 807 6813

Distributed in Australia by
Sandstone Publishing
Unit 1
360 Norton Street
Leichhardt
New South Wales 2040
tel. 02 9560 7888
fax 02 9560 7488

1 3 5 7 9 10 8 6 4 2

Publisher: Joanna Lorenz
Senior Editor: Lindsay Porter
Designer: Lilian Lindblom
Photographer: Lizzie Orme
Stylist: Katie Gibbs
Illustrators: Madeleine David and Lucinda Ganderton

Previously published as *Inspirations: Stamping*

CONTENTS

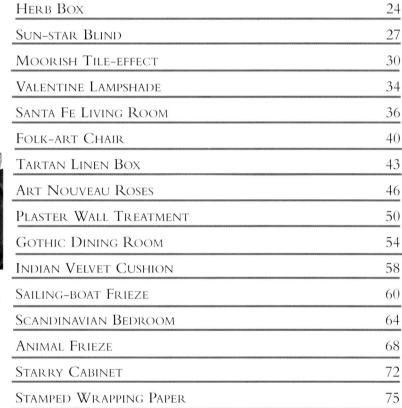

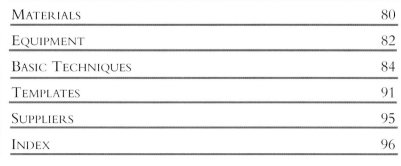

INTRODUCTION

Most of us first encountered stamping as children when we made potato-print cards at school. They may have been a little rough around the edges but they were so easy to do. Stamping in your own home is just as simple, although the results are often quite sophisticated. You can make your own customized stamps from potatoes or ordinary household sponges. Alternatively, commercial stamps are available in a variety of sizes and designs.

Although stamping is sometimes thought of as another form of stencilling, it is essentially a form of printing, which means that the finished effect is very different from a stencilled design. Stamping can add detail to almost any surface – from walls to wrapping paper – as long as it is firm enough for you to apply the pressure to form the print. With practice, you can even stamp around curves. Once you have made your basic stamped pattern, it is possible to add extra details with freehand painting, or to add colour to the design.

With over 20 projects in this book there is bound to be a project to suit your home. We have also included a comprehensive section of basic techniques, as well as stamp effects that will add an extra dimension to your work, such as the art of creating subtle highlights and shadows. All the patterns for the stamps are included, together with information on materials required. Techniques and projects are fully illustrated with clear, easy-to-follow step-by-step photography. For successful results, remember to hold the stamp steady while you work and do not let it move or slide, be confident, and practise on a sheet of scrap paper before you begin. So get stamping – once you have mastered the essentials, you can use your new-found skills to transform your home.

Deborah Barker

FLOWER-POT FRIEZE

This witty frieze has a 1950s feel and creates an eye-catching feature above a half-boarded wall. Use scraps of leftover wallpaper or sheets of wrapping paper for the pots, and stamp an exuberant display of flowers around your kitchen.

YOU WILL NEED
matt emulsion (latex) paints in pale blue and white
broad and fine paintbrushes
old cloth
pencil
wallpaper or wrapping paper
scissors
PVA (white) glue
green acrylic paint
stamp inkpads in a variety of colours
large and small daisy rubber stamps
cotton wool buds (swabs)
scrap paper

1 Paint tongue-and-groove boarding or the lower half of the wall with pale blue emulsion (latex) paint and leave to dry.

2 Using a dry paintbrush, lightly brush white emulsion over the flat colour. For a softer effect, rub the paint in with an old cloth.

3 To make the frieze, draw flower-pot shapes on to scraps of different wallpapers or wrapping papers and cut them out. Cut scalloped strips of paper and glue one along the top of each flower pot, using PVA (white) glue.

4 Glue the flower pots along the wall, at evenly spaced intervals.

5 Using acrylic paint and a fine paintbrush, paint green stems coming out of each pot. Leave the paint to dry before beginning to print the flowers.

6 Use coloured inkpads to ink the daisy stamps, using the lighter colours first. To ink the flower centre in a different colour, remove the first colour from the centre using a cotton wool bud (swab), then use a small inkpad to dab on the second colour.

7 Test the stamp on a sheet of scrap paper before applying it to the wall.

▶

8 Print the lighter-coloured flowers on the ends of some of the stems, using large and small daisy stamps. Allow the ink to dry.

9 Print the darker flowers on the remaining stems. Allow the flowers to overlap to create full, blossoming pots.

GRAPE-VINE FRIEZE AND GLASSES

This elegant repeating design is a combination of sponging and freehand painting – practise the strokes on paper before embarking on the wall, and keep your hand relaxed to make confident, sweeping lines. It's perfect for a kitchen or conservatory and is repeated on a set of glasses to carry the theme on to the table.

YOU WILL NEED
medium-density sponge, such as a kitchen sponge
marker pen
small coin
scissors or craft knife and cutting mat
ruler
pencil
acrylic paints in purple and blue
paint-mixing container
medium and fine paintbrushes
glasses
kitchen cloth
ceramic paints in purple and blue

1 Copy the template at the back of the book and use to draw the leaf shape on a piece of medium-density sponge. To make the stamp for the grapes, draw around a coin, or copy the grape template.

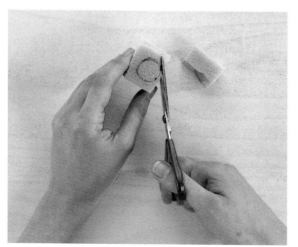

2 Cut out the sponge shapes using a pair of scissors or craft knife.

3 Trace the template of the frieze design on to the wall, carefully marking the positions of the grapes and leaves.

4 Mix up two shades of purple acrylic paint. Using a paintbrush, load one side of the grape stamp with dark purple and the other with a lighter shade to give a shadowed effect.

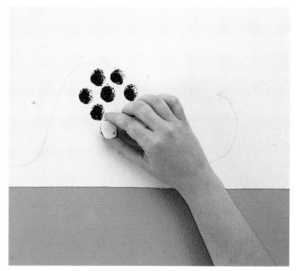

5 Build up the bunch of grapes, starting with the top row and working downwards to avoid smudges. Position the grapes in succeeding rows diagonally between the ones above. Keep the dark side of each grape facing the same way.

6 Mix up two shades of blue paint and load the leaf stamp, painting the outside edge in the darker shade. Stamp the leaf shape where marked on either side of each bunch of grapes. Paint the stems free-hand in the lighter shade of blue, using a fine brush.

7 Before decorating the glasses with the grape motif, clean each thoroughly to remove any trace of grease. Leave to dry.

▶

8 Mix two shades of purple ceramic paint and load the grape stamp as before. Align the first row of grapes below the edge of the glass, keeping clear of the rim.

9 Build up the bunch of grapes so that it fills one side of the glass.

10 Mix two shades of blue ceramic paint and load the leaf stamp as before. Stamp a leaf motif on either side of the bunch of grapes.

11 Paint the stems in the lighter shade of blue, using a fine brush. Leave the glass for 24 hours to dry completely. The glasses will withstand gentle washing but should not be put in a dishwasher or cleaned with an abrasive scourer.

MEXICAN-STYLE CHOPPING BOARDS

Commercially available woodstains tend to be dull, but it's easy to mix up your own vivid woodwashes using acrylic paints to brighten up plain kitchen utensils, before decorating them with vegetable motifs in hot colours. Rubber stamps are available in thousands of designs and produce sharp and detailed results, which you can then colour by hand.

YOU WILL NEED
acrylic paints in red, yellow, yellow ochre and lime green
paint-mixing container
medium paintbrush
wooden chopping boards
old cloth
rubber stamps in tomato, chilli or other vegetable designs
black stamp inkpad
permanent marker pens in red and green
clear wax
soft cloth

1 For the orange board, mix up a woodwash using 5ml/1 tsp of the first three acrylic colours, blended with water to the consistency of single (light) cream. Paint the wash on to the wood, following the direction of the grain.

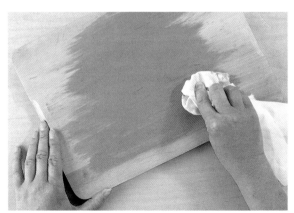

2 Wipe off the excess paint using a cloth, again following the direction of the grain. Repeat on the back and sides of the board. Allow to dry. ▶

3 Using rubber stamps and a black inkpad, print a different vegetable motif carefully in each corner of the board.

4 When the ink has dried, hand-tint each motif using permanent marker pens.

5 To seal the wood, rub on a layer of clear wax with a soft cloth. Repeat the procedure with a wash of lime green and the same motifs for the second board.

STRAWBERRY TRUG

Strawberry motifs always look fresh and pretty, with their bright red fruits and shapely leaves, and the sponging technique used here suits the texture of strawberries particularly well. This decorative planter would look lovely on a kitchen windowsill filled with herbs, or, of course, with strawberry plants.

YOU WILL NEED
medium-grade sandpaper
wooden planter
broad, medium and fine paintbrushes
white matt emulsion (latex) paint
medium-density sponge, such as a kitchen sponge
marker pen
scissors or craft knife and cutting mat
pencil
acrylic paints in red, green and yellow
paint-mixing container
clear acrylic varnish

1 Lightly sand the wooden planter to prepare the surface for painting.

2 Apply two coats of white emulsion paint, allowing the paint to dry and sanding lightly between coats.

3 Copy the strawberry, leaf and calyx designs from the back of the book. Draw around them on the sponge with a marker pen and cut away the sponge around the shapes using scissors or a craft knife and cutting mat.

4 Mark the positions of the strawberries on the planter. Load the strawberry stamp with red acrylic paint, then stamp the strawberries on the planter. Allow to dry.

▶

19

5 Load the calyx stamp with green acrylic paint and stamp just above the strawberry shapes.

6 Mark the positions of the large and small leaves on the planter. Load the leaf stamp with green paint and stamp the leaves, making the large leaves by stamping three times.

7 Allow the leaves to dry, then use a pencil to mark the positions of the stems and paint them free-hand using a fine paintbrush and green paint.

8 Use a fine paintbrush to paint yellow seeds on the strawberries. When the paint is dry, apply two coats of acrylic varnish to protect the design.

SPOTTED FLOWER POTS

Customized terracotta pots will give a new, fresh look to your conservatory, patio or kitchen windowsill. Light, bright colours suit this pattern really well, but you can make them as subtle or as bold as you please. The end of a small sponge roller gives a neat, sharp image.

YOU WILL NEED
terracotta flower pots
white acrylic primer
medium paintbrushes
matt emulsion (latex) paints in a variety
of colours including yellow, white, red
and blue
paint-mixing container
old plate
small sponge paint rollers
satin acrylic varnish

1 Make sure the flower pots are clean and dry. Prime them with a coat of white acrylic primer and leave to dry.

2 Dilute some yellow emulsion (latex) paint with water to the consistency of single (light) cream. Colourwash the first pot using a dry brush and random brush strokes. Allow to dry.

3 Spread some white paint over an old plate. Press the end of a small sponge paint roller into the paint, ensuring that it is totally covered, then press it firmly on to the first flower pot. Remove carefully and repeat all over the pot. Allow to dry.

4 Repeat using red paint over half the white spots, but position the sponge slightly to one side of each white spot to give a highlighted three-dimensional effect. Colour the rest of the spots blue. Leave to dry.

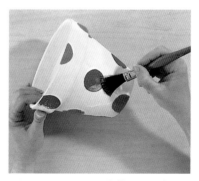

5 Repeat using different colour combinations on the other pots. Seal the pots with 2–3 thin, even coats of satin acrylic varnish, allowing the varnish to dry between coats.

HERB BOX

A miniature chest of drawers with decorations on a botanical theme makes a charming store for dried herbs in the pantry, or would look equally good in the potting shed, filled with seeds. Small, unpainted wooden chests are inexpensive and widely available.

YOU WILL NEED
unpainted wooden chest of drawers
6 unpainted wooden knobs with screws
white acrylic primer
medium paintbrushes
matt emulsion (latex) paints in two shades of pale green
clear wax
medium-grade sandpaper
ruler
pencil
drill and drill bit
rubber stamps in plant designs
green stamp inkpad
screwdriver

1 Prime the chest, drawers and knobs with an even coat of white acrylic primer. Allow to dry. If the drawers have thumb-holes in their fronts, as here, reverse them.

2 Paint the chest, drawers and knobs in pale green and leave to dry thoroughly.

3 Apply clear wax to the edges and corners, wherever the chest and knobs would receive most natural wear and tear. Allow to set for 10 minutes.

4 Paint on a coat of very pale green and allow to dry.

▶

5 Using medium-grade sandpaper, rub down the areas where the wax was applied to reveal the base colour.

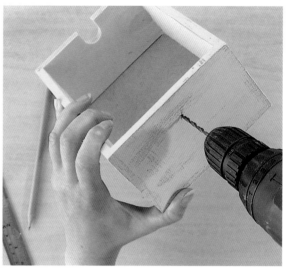

6 Mark each drawer 2.5cm/1in down from the centre top and drill a hole for the knob.

7 Ink a rubber stamp using the inkpad and press on to the drawer below the drilled hole. Choose a different herb or flower design for each drawer.

8 When the stamped designs are dry, screw the knobs to the drawers.

SUN-STAR BLIND

Turn a plain white blind into a chic window dressing by colourwashing it to give a pretty, cloudy effect, then adding a vibrant pattern of stamped motifs. Fix on an ornate blind-pull or tassel to give the finishing touch to the transformation.

YOU WILL NEED

matt emulsion (latex) paints in purple and yellow
acrylic scumble glaze
paint-mixing container
medium paintbrush
plain white roller blind
natural sponge
marker pens in black and gold
paper
scissors
12.5cm/5in square of high density sponge, such as upholstery foam (foam rubber)
craft knife and cutting mat
old plate
bradawl
brass screw eye
blind-pull or tassel

1 Mix some purple emulsion (latex) paint with acrylic scumble glaze. Lay the blind on a flat surface. Dip a natural sponge into the paint and wipe the colour over the blind in a circular motion to give a soft, cloudy effect. Allow to dry.

2 Draw the sun-star design freehand on to a piece of paper and cut it out. Trace around the shape to a square of high-density sponge. Cut out using a craft knife.

3 Spread some yellow emulsion paint over an old plate. Press the sponge on to the paint, making sure the surface is entirely covered, then on to the blind. Repeat, spacing the sun-star evenly and over-lapping the edges of the blind. Allow to dry. ▶

4 Outline each shape and draw in the details using a gold marker pen.

5 Make a hole in the centre of the bottom batten using a bradawl and screw in a small brass eye. Attach a decorative blind-pull or tassel.

MOORISH TILE-EFFECT

*Moorish wall patterns are based on abstract, geometric motifs which you can reproduce most
effectively with stamps. In this wall treatment, a lozenge shape is incorporated in a subtle
tile design on a cool colourwashed background.*

YOU WILL NEED
matt emulsion (latex) paints in mid-blue, off-white and terracotta
wallpaper paste
paint-mixing container
broad and fine paintbrushes
thin card (cardboard)
ruler
pencil
scissors
medium-density sponge, such as a kitchen sponge
marker pen
craft knife and cutting mat
spirit level (carpenter's level)

1 Mix the mid-blue emulsion (latex) with 50%
wallpaper paste and apply to the walls with a
broad brush, working at random angles and blending
the brushstrokes to avoid any hard edges.

2 Mix the off-white emulsion with 75% wallpaper
paste and brush on to the walls as before, to
soften the effect. Allow to dry.

3 To make a template for the tile shape, cut out a
30cm/12in square of thin card (cardboard).

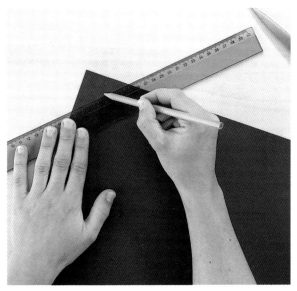

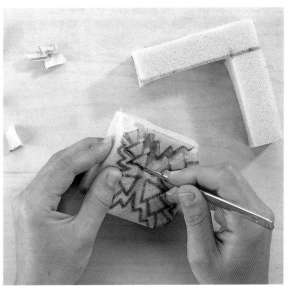

4 Mark the sides of the square 5cm/2in from each corner, draw a line across the diagonal and cut off the corners.

5 Copy the template from the back of the book and transfer it to a 5cm/2in square of medium-density sponge using a marker pen. Cut away the excess sponge using a craft knife.

6 Using a spirit level (carpenter's level), draw a horizontal line around the room where you want the top of the pattern. Place the top of the card template against the line and draw around it. Repeat over the pattern area.

7 Use paintbrushes to load the stamp with mid-blue and terracotta emulsion paint and print the motif in the diamond shapes created by the template.

▶

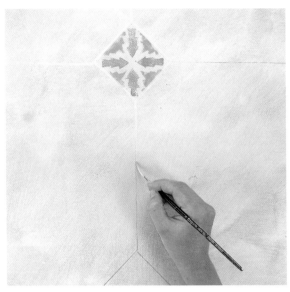

8 Dilute off-white emulsion with enough water to give the consistency of thick cream and use a fine paintbrush to paint over the pencil lines.

VALENTINE LAMPSHADE

*Contemporary yet romantic, this easy decorating idea turns a plain coolie lampshade into
an original feature. The sponging technique gives a softly mottled effect to the little hearts,
which are then defined with a sparkling freehand outline in gold.*

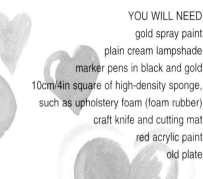

YOU WILL NEED
gold spray paint
plain cream lampshade
marker pens in black and gold
10cm/4in square of high-density sponge,
such as upholstery foam (foam rubber)
craft knife and cutting mat
red acrylic paint
old plate

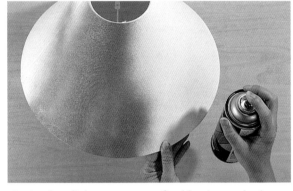

1 Apply a light, even coat of gold paint to the lampshade, holding the paint can about 25cm/10in from the surface and spraying in sweeping strokes. Leave to dry.

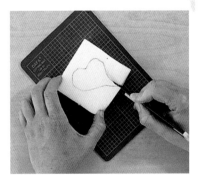

2 Using a marker pen, draw a freehand heart shape on a piece of high-density sponge and cut out using a craft knife.

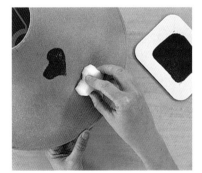

3 Spread some red acrylic paint over an old plate. Press the sponge on to the paint, making sure that the surface is entirely covered, then on to the lampshade. Repeat to create an all-over design, spacing the hearts evenly and overlapping the edges of the shade. Allow to dry.

4 Outline each heart shape using a gold marker pen.

SANTA FE LIVING ROOM

Aztec motifs, like this bird, are bold, stylized and one-dimensional, and translate perfectly into stamps. Strong colour contrasts suit this style, but here the pattern is confined to widely spaced stripes over a cool white wall, and further restrained with a final light wash of white paint.

YOU WILL NEED

matt emulsion (latex) paints in off-white, warm white, deep red
and navy blue
paint-mixing container
natural sponge
broad and medium paintbrushes
plumbline
ruler
pencil
masking tape
marker pen
medium-density sponge, such as a household sponge
craft knife and cutting mat
small paint roller
old plate
high-density sponge, such as upholstery foam (foam rubber)

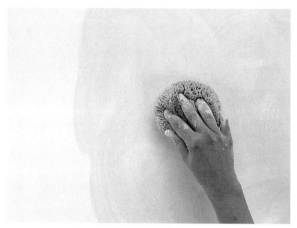

1 Dilute the off-white emulsion (latex) with 50% water and apply a wash over the wall using a sponge, alternating the angle at which you work. Allow to dry.

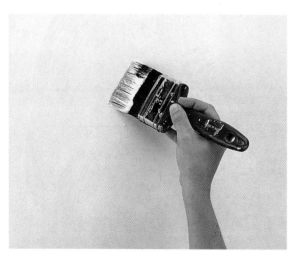

2 Using a broad, dry brush, apply warm white emulsion in some areas of the wall to achieve a rough-looking surface. Allow to dry.

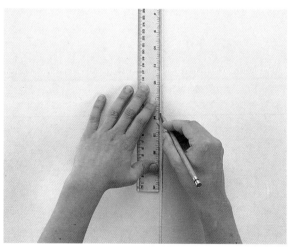

3 Starting 10cm/4in from one corner, and using a plumbline as a guide, draw a straight line from the top to the bottom of the wall.

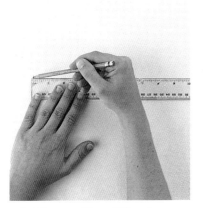

4 Measure 45cm/18in along the wall, hang the plumbline again and mark a second vertical line. Draw another line 10cm/4in away to create a band. Repeat all across the wall.

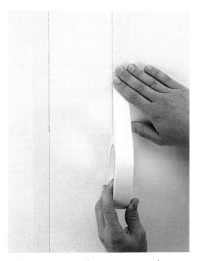

5 Apply masking tape to the wall on each outer edge of the marked bands.

6 Paint the bands in deep red emulsion. Leave to dry.

7 Draw a 10 x 20cm/4 x 8in diamond shape on a medium-density sponge and cut out the shape using a craft knife and cutting mat.

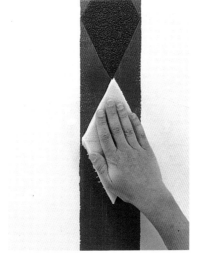

8 Use a small roller to load the stamp with navy blue emulsion paint and stamp the diamonds down the red bands, starting from the top and just touching at their tips.

9 Copy the bird template at the back of the book on to a piece of high-density sponge. Cut away the excess sponge using a craft knife.

▶

10 Use the roller to load the bird stamp with off-white emulsion and print the birds upright, roughly in the centre of the diamonds.

11 When the motifs are dry, use minimal pressure and a dry brush to brush gently over each band with warm white emulsion.

FOLK-ART CHAIR

Simple repeating designs on a white painted chair have a wonderfully naïve charm. Stick to a few bright colours in keeping with the folk-art style of this design, which any slight irregularities in the stamping will only serve to enhance.

YOU WILL NEED
medium-grade sandpaper
wooden chair
white matt emulsion (latex) paint
medium paintbrushes
pencil
scissors
medium-density sponge, such as a kitchen sponge
marker pen
coin
cork from a wine bottle
craft knife and cutting mat
ruler
acrylic paints in black, red, terracotta and blue
paint-mixing container
scrap paper
clear acrylic varnish

1 Sand the chair to remove any rough patches or old paint or varnish.

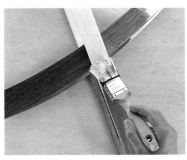

2 Paint the chair with two coats of white emulsion (latex) paint, allowing the paint to dry between coats.

3 Copy the designs from the back of the book and cut out paper templates of the heart and leaf shapes. Draw around the templates on to the sponge using a marker pen. Draw around a coin on the end of a cork to make the spot stamp.

4 Cut out the excess sponge and cork around the motifs using a craft knife.

▶

41

5 Using a pencil and ruler, mark the positions of the leaves, 6cm/2⅛in apart, on the struts of the chair back and seat.

6 Load the leaf stamp with black acrylic paint, then stamp once on a piece of scrap paper to remove excess paint. Stamp along the struts at a 45° angle. Alternate the direction of the leaves on each strut.

7 Load the heart stamp with red acrylic paint, remove the excess paint as before and stamp a heart at the top of each vertical strut, across the back and front of the chair.

8 Load the cork with terracotta acrylic paint, remove the excess paint as before and stamp a dot between each leaf shape.

9 Wash the terracotta paint off the cork, load it with blue and stamp dots 2cm/¾in apart along the legs and all round the edge of the chair.

10 Leave the paint to dry, then apply two coats of varnish to protect the design.

TARTAN LINEN BOX

Square and rectangular stamps take only a few seconds to cut, but here they have been cleverly combined to make a stylish plaid design. Use it to decorate a linen or calico-covered box like this one, or print the same pattern on to a wooden trunk, adding a coat of varnish for a hard-wearing finish.

YOU WILL NEED
ruler
plain fabric-covered box
graph paper
pencil
tailor's chalk
medium-density sponge, such as a kitchen sponge
marker pen
craft knife and cutting mat
acrylic paints in white and dark blue
paint-mixing container
medium paintbrush

1 Measure the top and sides of the box and transfer the measurements to a sheet of graph paper, using one square to represent 1cm/½in. Work out the design to fit the shapes, then scale up the grid and mark it in chalk on the box.

2 Make the stamps from medium–density sponge: using a marker pen, draw a long rectangle, a large square and a small square to fit your marked grid.

3 Cut out the shapes using a craft knife.

4 Using a paintbrush, load the rectangular stamp with white acrylic paint.

▶

5 Position the stamp between the chalked guidelines and press down gently. Repeat over the top and sides of the box.

6 Mix some mid-blue paint and use it to load the larger square. Print the stamp to form squares around alternate intersections on the grid.

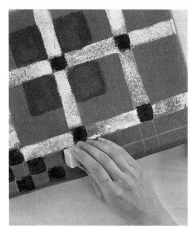

7 Load the small square with dark blue paint and stamp each intersection, then add a chequered border at each end of the lid and along the sides of the box.

8 Stamp dark blue squares, evenly spaced around the edge of the lid to complete the decoration.

ART NOUVEAU ROSES

This stylized, flowing design is inspired by the rose motif found in the work of Charles Rennie Mackintosh, who used it repeatedly in his interior designs, on chairs, doors, leaded glass and textiles. Used here to link a chair with the wall behind it, it is equally effective as a single motif or as a repeating pattern.

YOU WILL NEED
pencil
scissors
high-density sponge, such as upholstery foam (foam rubber)
craft knife and cutting mat
ruler
stiff card (cardboard)
PVA (white) glue
medium paintbrushes
marker pen
coin
acrylic paints in pink and green
director's chair with calico cover
tailor's chalk
fabric paints in green and pink

1 Scale up the designs at the back of the book to the size you require and make templates. Cut a square of sponge to fit the rose and a rectangle for the stem. Cut two pieces of card (cardboard) to fit the sponge shapes and glue them on.

2 Using a marker pen, transfer the designs to the sponge by drawing around the templates. Mark the top of each design on the card at the back.

3 Cut away the excess sponge from around the motifs using a craft knife. Make the stamp for the small dots by drawing around a coin and cutting out.

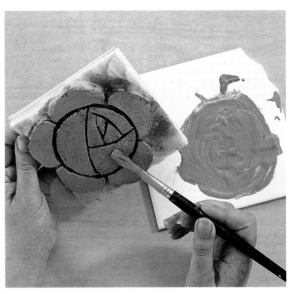

4 Using a pencil and ruler, and with the large stamp as a size guide, mark the positions of the bottom edges of the roses and stems on the wall, keeping the line parallel with the dado rail (chair rail). Repeat for the upper line of roses, then mark the centres of the small dots directly above the lower ones, and on a line equidistant from the two rows of roses.

5 Load the rose stamp with pink acrylic paint.

6 Match the bottom edge of the stamp to the marked wall and apply the stamp.

7 Load the small dot with green acrylic paint and stamp at the marked points. ▶

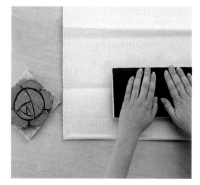

8 Load the stem stamp with green paint and stamp at the marked points. Repeat to complete the rows.

9 Remove the cover from the back of the chair and lay it out flat. Using chalk, mark the positions for the motifs along a line 5cm/2in in from each side. Load the stem stamp with green fabric paint and position the bottom edge on the marked line.

10 Load the rose stamp with pink fabric paint to complete the stamped design. Leave to dry, then rub off the chalk marks and fix the fabric paints according to the manufacturer's instructions.

PLASTER WALL TREATMENT

Add an extra dimension to stamping and create a relief effect on your walls. For this technique, a mixture of paint and interior filler (spackle) is applied to the stamp and then pressed on to the wall, leaving a raised motif. A monochromatic scheme suits this look best.

YOU WILL NEED

matt emulsion (latex) paints in off-white, lime white and
stone white
wallpaper paste
paint-mixing container
broad and medium paintbrushes
45cm/18in square card (cardboard)
pencil
high-density sponge, such as upholstery foam (foam rubber)
marker pen or white crayon
craft knife and cutting mat
interior filler (spackle)

1 Mix the off-white emulsion (latex) with 50% wallpaper paste and apply to the walls with a broad paintbrush, working at random angles and keeping the effect quite rough.

2 Apply random patches of lime white, allowing the basecoat to show in areas.

3 Using the card (cardboard) square as a template and beginning in a corner of the room, make a small mark at each corner of the card. Reposition the card using the previous marks as a guide and repeat to form a grid of evenly spaced marks around the room.

4 Copy the template at the back of the book and transfer it to a piece of high-density sponge. Cut away the excess sponge using a craft knife.

5 Mix stone white emulsion with interior filler (spackle), using about one part filler to three parts paint.

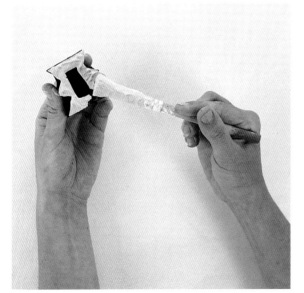

6 Apply the mixture thickly to the stamp using a dabbing motion.

7 Print over each pencil mark, pressing the stamp quite hard and pulling it cleanly away – be careful not to smear the impression. Leave for about 4 hours to dry.

8 Dry brush a little lime white emulsion over each stamp, so that only the areas in highest relief pick up the paint.

GOTHIC DINING ROOM

Create a dramatic setting for candlelit dinner parties with purple and gold panels that will shimmer from deep velvety green walls. The effect is achieved by stamping the wall with gold size and then rubbing on Dutch gold leaf which will adhere to the stamped motifs.

YOU WILL NEED
30cm/12in square thin card (cardboard)
ruler
pencil
scissors
high-density sponge, such as upholstery foam (foam rubber)
marker pen
craft knife and cutting mat
matt emulsion (latex) paints in dark green and purple
natural sponge
plumbline
small paint roller
old plate
gold size
Dutch gold leaf
soft brush

1 To make a template for the wall panels, draw a freehand arc from the centre top of the card (cardboard) square to the lower corner.

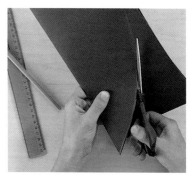

2 Fold the card in half down the centre and cut out both sides to make a symmetrical Gothic arch shape.

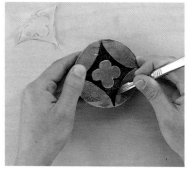

3 Copy the design from the back of the book and make a paper pattern with a diameter of 10cm/4in. Transfer the design on to a piece of high-density sponge. Cut away the excess sponge using a craft knife.

4 Apply dark green emulsion (latex) liberally to the wall, using a sponge and working in a circular motion. Allow to dry.

5 Using a plumbline as a guide and beginning 23cm/9in from a corner, mark a vertical line up the wall to a height of 1.8m/6ft.

6 Measure across the wall and use the plumbline to draw vertical lines every 60cm/2ft.

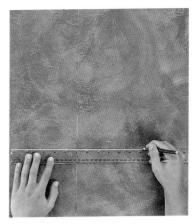

7 Measure out 15cm/6in each side of each vertical and draw two more lines to mark the edges of the panels.

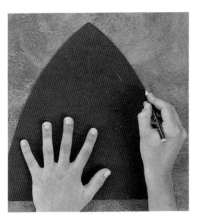

8 Place the point of the card template at the centre top point of each panel and draw in the curves.

9 Use a small paint roller to load the stamp with gold size and print each panel, beginning with the centre top and working down the central line, then down each side.

10 When the size is tacky, apply Dutch gold leaf by rubbing over the backing paper with a soft brush.

▶

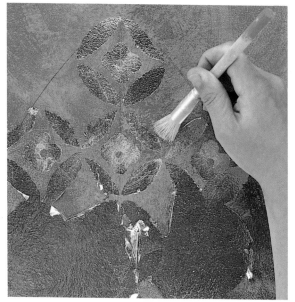

11 Once the panel is complete, use a soft brush to remove any excess gold leaf.

12 Using only the centre of the stamp, fill in the spaces between the gold motifs using purple emulsion paint.

INDIAN VELVET CUSHION

Indian textile printing blocks are available in numerous designs. This is an opulent way to decorate cushions or other fabric accessories. Add metallic powders to fabric-painting medium to give a glittery effect with a hard-wearing finish.

YOU WILL NEED
150cm/1½yd velvet
tape measure
scissors
dressmaker's pins
sewing machine and matching sewing thread
4 gold tassels
bronze powder
fabric-painting medium
paint-mixing container
medium paintbrush
scrap paper
Indian textile printing block
3 gold buttons
sewing needle
56cm/22in cushion pad

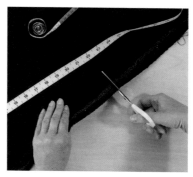

1 Cut out a 58cm/23in square and two rectangles 33 x 58cm/ 13 x 23in from the velvet.

2 To make the back of the cushion, turn in, pin and stitch a double hem along one long edge of each rectangle. Make three buttonholes, evenly spaced, in the hem of one piece.

3 Right sides together, pin the buttonholed piece to the square front on three sides. Pin the second back piece on top, stitched hems overlapping. Insert a tassel in the seam at each corner, facing in. Stitch and turn through. Flatten the seams and lay the cushion on a flat surface.

4 Add one part bronze powder to two parts fabric-painting medium and mix thoroughly. Insert scrap paper inside the cushion. Paint an even coat of the mixture on to the block. Position the block along one edge of the cushion and press down firmly. Repeat to complete the design.

5 Remove the scrap paper. Sew a gold button opposite each buttonhole on the back of the cushion cover. Insert the pad and fasten the buttons.

SAILING-BOAT FRIEZE

Use this charming yacht bobbing on the waves to complete a bathroom with a nautical theme.
It is better, if possible, to stamp tiles before fixing them to the wall, so that the ceramic paints
can be made more resilient by baking in the oven. You can stamp and appliqué the same design,
with embroidered details, on to your towels.

YOU WILL NEED
high-density sponge, such as
upholstery foam (foam rubber)
craft knife and cutting mat
ruler
stiff card (cardboard)
PVA (white) glue
medium paintbrush
pencil
scissors
marker pen
ceramic paints in
various colours
paint-mixing container
15cm/6in square ceramic tiles
old cloth
methylated spirits (rubbing
alcohol)
plain light-coloured cotton fabric
masking tape
fabric paints
embroidery hoop
stranded embroidery thread
sewing needle
dressmaker's pins
hand towel
8 pearl buttons

1 Cut a 15cm/6in square and a 15 x 5 cm/6 x 2in rectangle of sponge to make the stamps. Cut a piece of card (cardboard) for each square and glue one on to each sponge.

2 Scale up the designs at the back of the book to fit a 15cm/6in tile and make paper templates. Draw around the boat and wave designs on the square stamp using a marker pen.

3 Cut away the excess sponge around the design using a craft knife. Repeat on the rectangular sponge to make the second stamp, positioning the waves so that they will fall between the first set.

4 Load the boat stamp with ceramic paints, applying the colours to the different areas using a paintbrush.Clean any grease from the surface of the tiles by rubbing with a cloth dipped in methylated spirits (rubbing alcohol). Allow to dry.

5 Press the stamp over the tile. Allow to dry. Load the waves stamp and stamp another set of waves between the first set.

6 For the wave tiles, re-load the wave stamp with paint and position it 1 cm/½in from the bottom edge. Apply the stamp, aligning it with the bottom edge. Print birds at a 45° angle above the waves.

Above: Using the same design on your tilework and linen adds a pleasing unity to your bathroom's interior design. ▶

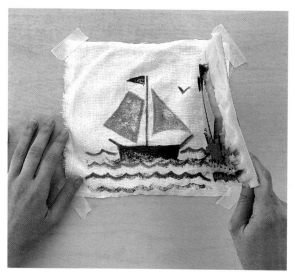

7 For the appliqué towel panel, cut out a 17cm/7in square of fabric and tape it to the work surface. Mix fabric paints to match the ceramic paint colours and load the boat motif as before. Stamp on to the fabric and leave to dry.

8 Fix the paints according to the manufacturer's instructions, then insert the panel in an embroidery hoop and work a running stitch to pick out the clouds and details on the sail and boat in stranded embroidery thread.

9 Press under a 1 cm/½in hem all round the panel and pin it in place at one end of the towel. Work a blanket stitch all round the panel to attach it.

10 Stitch a pearl button to each corner of the panel, and one in the middle of each side.

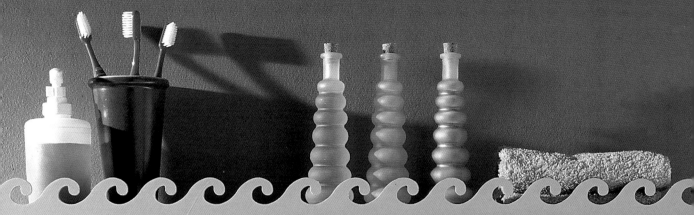

SCANDINAVIAN BEDROOM

This delicate stamped decoration on walls and woodwork is designed to go with the pale colours and painted furniture that characterize period Scandinavian interiors. This is a scheme of great charm, restful on the eye and perfect for a bedroom.

YOU WILL NEED
matt emulsion (latex) paints in grey blue,
off-white and red
paint-mixing container
wallpaper paste
broad and fine paintbrushes
plumbline
ruler
pencil
marker pen or white crayon
high-density sponge, such as
upholstery foam (foam rubber)
craft knife and cutting mat
small paint roller
old plate
matt acrylic varnish

1 Mix the grey-blue emulsion (latex) with 50% wallpaper paste and apply to the walls with a broad paintbrush, working at random angles and blending the brushstrokes to avoid hard edges.

2 Allow to dry, then repeat the process to soften the effect.

3 Mix the off-white emulsion with 75% wallpaper paste and brush on to the walls as before. Allow to dry.

4 Hang a plumbline 2.5cm/1in from one corner and use as a guide to draw a vertical line down the wall.

5 Measure about 40cm/16in across and draw a second vertical line, again using the plumbline as a guide. Repeat all around the room.

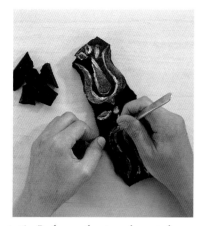

6 Scale up the template at the back of the book and draw it on a rectangle of high-density sponge. Cut away the excess sponge around the design using a craft knife.

7 Use a small paint roller to load the stamp with off-white emulsion paint.

8 Add details in red and grey-blue emulsion, using a paintbrush to add the colours over the off-white paint.

9 Apply the stamp to the wall, positioning it centrally over the marked line.

10 Repeat, positioning the stamp so that each motif is just touching the preceding one. Work down from the top of the wall.

11 Use the grey-blue wash mixed for the wall basecoat to drag the door: applying pressure to the bristles, pull down in a straight line, following the direction of the wood grain.

12 Apply the paint to the stamp as before, but this time loading only one flower motif. Stamp a single motif diagonally into the corners of each door panel.

13 Add more paint to the grey-blue wash to deepen the colour and use it to edge the door panels. Leave to dry, then apply two coats of matt varnish to the door to protect the design.

ANIMAL FRIEZE

A low frieze is perfect for a nursery as it concentrates interest at the child's own level. Children can't fail to be enchanted by this harmonious troop of animals all sharing the same flowery field, with clouds billowing overhead.

YOU WILL NEED

emulsion (latex) paints in sky blue, grass green, yellow and white
paint roller
broad and fine paintbrushes
paint-mixing container
stamp inkpads in a variety of colours
rubber stamps in cow, chicken, pig and sheep designs
natural sponge

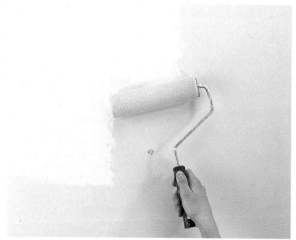

1 Paint the wall in sky blue emulsion (latex) and allow to dry.

2 Paint the skirting-board (baseboard) in a grass green.

3 Using the same green paint, apply wispy strokes up the wall to create the effect of grass. Allow the paint to dry.

4 Using a finer paintbrush, highlight the grass with a lighter, yellowy green.

5 Paint small daisies in white emulsion at random in the grass. Add yellow centres.

6 Using a black inkpad, stamp the cow at random along the frieze.

7 Print groups of chickens, using brown ink.

8 Print the pig, using pink ink.

9 Print the sheep, using black ink. Using a fine paintbrush, fill in the body of the sheep in white emulsion paint. Do the same with the cow if you wish.

10 Lightly press a natural sponge into white emulsion paint and sponge cloud shapes on the sky blue wall above the frieze.

STARRY CABINET

Turn a small junk-shop find into a unique bedside cabinet using a palette of fresh colours and a simple star motif. Before you start to paint, divide the piece visually into blocks, each of which will be a different colour, with a further shade for the frame. Keep all the colours in similar tones to achieve this pretty, sugared-almond effect.

YOU WILL NEED
medium-grade sandpaper
wooden cabinet
wood filler
acrylic wood primer
medium and fine paintbrushes
emulsion (latex) paints in green, pink, blue and yellow
wooden knobs
star rubber stamp
stamp inkpads in a variety of colours
drill and drill bit
screwdriver and screws
masking tape
acrylic spray varnish

1 Sand the cabinet to remove any rough patches or old paint or varnish. Fill any holes with wood filler and sand down. Paint the wood with a coat of primer and leave to dry.

2 Paint the cabinet using different coloured emulsion (latex) paints and allow to dry.

3 Using an assortment of all the colours except that of the frame, paint a row of spots around the frame. ▶

4 Paint the wooden knobs and, when the paint has dried, stamp a contrasting star motif on each one using coloured inkpads. When dry, drill screw holes and screw the knobs into position.

5 Stamp a contrasting star motif on to each of the spots around the cabinet frame.

6 Use masking tape to mark out a row of stripes along the bottom of the cabinet and paint them in a contrasting colour.

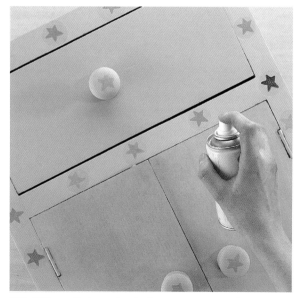

7 When all the paint is dry, protect it with a coat of acrylic spray varnish. Leave to dry thoroughly.

STAMPED WRAPPING PAPER

You can turn plain sheets of paper into fabulous hand-printed gift wrap using simple, bold lino-cut motifs and coloured inks. The designs are finished off using small rubber stamps. For the chequerboard design, position the lino block carefully to get an even pattern. Cut up a large sheet to make gift tags, threaded with narrow ribbon.

YOU WILL NEED
linoleum board
marker pen
wood offcut
lino-cutting tools
water-soluble printing ink in a variety of colours
small pane of glass or old saucer
rubber ink roller
wrapping paper
metal spoon
small star and spot rubber stamps
stamp inkpads in a variety of colours

1 Draw the star and star outline freehand onto paper. Cut out and copy on to two squares of lino, using a marker pen.

2 Butt the first lino square against an offcut of wood and place that against a wall on a flat surface, to prevent the lino slipping. Cut away the area around the design using lino–cutting tools.

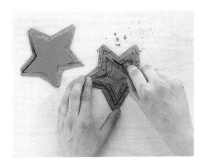

3 To cut out the spots for the star outline you will need a fine cutting tool. Place the point of the tool on a marked spot and scoop out the lino. Dust away the shavings.

4 Select a coloured ink for the star shape and squeeze a small amount on to a piece of glass or old saucer. Roll out the ink until it feels tacky, then roll it on to the star stamp. Do not apply too much or the lino will slip when printing. ▶

5 Position the star stamp on the paper and press down, holding firmly in place. Smooth the back of the lino with the back of a metal spoon. Reapply the ink before printing each star.

6 Use a darker shade of ink for the star outline and line it up carefully over the plain shape. Smooth over the back with a spoon as before, and print the outline over all the stars.

7 To complete the star design, use a small star-shaped rubber stamp and coloured inkpads to match the large stars. Apply the small stars at random between the large ones.

8 Follow the design in the picture to make a chequerboard stamp in the same way. Finish with a small spot-shaped rubber stamp on each square.

REGAL PHOTO ALBUM

Embossing stamped motifs is great fun and works like magic. It's used here to make a glittering gold crown that sits like a royal crest on an album cover. In its setting of tinsel, sequins and fake jewels, however, the effect is quirkily amusing rather than regal.

YOU WILL NEED
crown rubber stamp
embossing inkpad
coloured paper
gold embossing powder
scrap paper
toaster or oven ring (burner)
scissors
felt, in contrasting colours
PVA (white) glue
fine paintbrush
tinsel
sequins
plastic gemstones
photograph album
cylindrical container
gold braid

1 Press the stamp on to the embossing ink pad and stamp it on to a square of coloured paper. Immediately sprinkle the embossing powder all over the stamped image.

2 Shake off the excess powder on to scrap paper (pour the excess back into the container). Hold the design over a toaster or oven ring (burner) and watch the powder melt. This should take only a few seconds. Don't rest the paper on the heat source and don't leave it unattended. Allow to cool.

3 Cut four strips of contrasting felt to fit along each side of the paper. Snip out triangles to make a spiky border. Glue the felt strips to the paper and embellish them by gluing on tinsel and sequins.

4 Glue a plastic gemstone to each point of the crown, then glue the collage on to the front of the album.

5 To make a matching pencil pot (jar), stamp embossed crowns along a strip of paper to fit around a cylindrical container and glue it in place. Trim the top edge with a strip of braid decorated with sequins and gemstones.

MATERIALS

Different paints and stamps will produce very different results.

DUTCH METAL LEAF AND GOLD SIZE
Metal leaf is a cheap, easy-to-use alternative to real gold leaf. Use a sponge stamp to apply gold size in a repeating pattern. When the size is tacky, apply the gold leaf.

INKS
Water-based inks are too runny to use on their own but can be added to wallpaper paste or varnish to make a mixture thick enough to adhere to the stamp. Use them for paper or card, but not for walls. If you are using rubber stamps, inkpads are commercially available in a wide range of colours.

INTERIOR FILLER (SPACKLE)
Add filler, in its dry powdered state, to emulsion paint to give it body without diluting the colour.

PAINT
Water-based paints such as emulsion (latex) and artist's acrylics dry quickly to a perma-nent finish. Use emulsion paint straight from the can or dilute it with wallpaper paste or varnish. For wall treatments, emulsion paint can be thinned with water and sponged or brushed over the wall as a colourwash.

PRECUT STAMPS
Rubber stamps are widely avail-able in thousands of designs.

Finely detailed motifs are best suited to small-scale projects, while bolder shapes are best for walls and furniture.

SPONGE OR FOAM
Different types of sponge are characterized by their density. High-density sponge is best for detailed shapes and will give a smooth, sharp print. Medium-density sponge or low-density sponge will absorb more paint and give a more textured result.

VARNISH
Use water-based, acrylic varnish (sold as quick-drying) for stamping projects. It can be mixed with emulsion paint or ink to thicken the texture and create a range of different sheens.

WALLPAPER PASTE
Wallpaper paste allows you to thin emulsion paint without making it too runny to adhere to the stamp. Mix up the paste with the required amount of water first, then add the emulsion.

Opposite: Dutch metal leaf and gold size (1); coloured inks (2); low-density sponge (3); precut stamp (4); high-density sponge (5); medium-density sponges (6); interior filler (spackle) (7); emulsion (latex) paint (8); varnish (9); wallpaper paste (10).

8

EQUIPMENT

*Stamping does not require a great deal of specialist equipment;
many of the items used are found in most households.*

CRAFT KNIFE
A sharp-bladed craft knife is essential for cutting your own stamps out of sponge. Use a cutting mat to protect your work surface, and always direct the blade away from your fingers.

LINO BLOCKS
Lino blocks are available from art and craft shops and can be cut to make stamps which recreate the look of a wood block. You'll need special lino-cutting tools, which are also easily available, to scoop out the areas around the design. Always hold the lino with your spare hand behind your cutting hand for safety.

MASKING TAPE
Use for masking off areas of walls and furniture when painting.

NATURAL SPONGE
Use for applying colourwashes to walls before stamping.

PAINTBRUSHES
A range of decorator's brushes is needed for painting furniture and walls before stamping. Use a broad brush to apply colourwashes to walls. Stiff brushes can be used to stipple paint on to stamps for textured effects, while finer brushes are used to pick out details or to apply paint to the stamp.

PENCILS, PENS AND CRAYONS
Use a soft pencil to trace templates for stamps, and for making easily removable guidelines on walls. Draw motifs freehand using a marker pen on medium- and low-density sponge. Use a white crayon on black upholstery foam.

RAGS
Keep a stock of clean rags and cloths for cleaning stamps and preparing surfaces.

RULER AND TAPE MEASURE
Use these to plan your design.

SCISSORS
Use sharp scissors to cut out medium- and low-density sponge shapes and for cutting out templates.

SPONGE ROLLERS
Small paint rollers can be used to load your stamps. You will need several if you are stamping in different colours.

Opposite: scissors (1); craft knife (2); masking tape (3); paint rollers (4); ruler (5); tape measure (6); pencils (7); cutting mat (8); rag (9); natural sponge (10); paintbrushes (11).

BASIC TECHNIQUES

*Stamping is a quick and effective method of repeating a design on a wide variety of surfaces,
using many different mixtures of paints and inks. Ready-made stamps are widely available,
usually mounted on wooden blocks, but they are also easy to make yourself using foam or sponge.*

MAKING STAMPS

1 Use high-density sponge for sharply defined and detailed designs. Trace your chosen motif on to the sponge using a soft pencil for dark, clear lines.

2 Roughly cut around the design, then spray the tracing paper with adhesive to hold it in place on the sponge while you are cutting it out.

3 Cut along the outline using a sharp blade, then, pinching the background sections, cut them away holding the blade away from your fingers.

4 The surface of low-density sponge is too soft to use tracing paper; it is easier to draw the design straight on to the sponge using a marker pen.

5 Sharp scissors can be used with this material and are especially useful for cutting out the basic shapes.

6 As with high-density sponge, the unwanted background areas should be cut away with a craft knife when the outline has been cut, but care is needed as this sponge will tear more easily. Rinse the completed stamp to remove the remains of the marker ink.

PAINT MIXTURES

WALLPAPER PASTE AND EMULSION (LATEX) PAINT

Add 50% paste to the paint to give a watercolour effect without producing a mixture that is too runny to work with. Apply using a roller, sponge or paintbrush, or dip the stamp into the paint on a flat plate.

WALLPAPER PASTE AND INK

Wallpaper paste thickens the texture of ink, while keeping the rich colour. The effect produced depends on the proportion of ink in the mixture. It will give a more even spread of colour than using emulsion. Apply using a roller or paintbrush.

VARNISH AND EMULSION PAINT

The density of the paint is diluted as with wallpaper paste, but this can also be used to create different sheens according to the type of varnish used. Apply with a roller, paintbrush or sponge, or dip the stamp into the paint on a plate.

VARNISH AND INK

This effect is similar to the wallpaper paste mixture, but creates a smoother mix as both materials are fine in texture. Again, different sheens can be obtained. Apply with a roller.

WALLPAPER PASTE AND WOODSTAIN

The paste dilutes the colour density of the stain while thickening the mixture for ease of use. Use quick-drying, water-based woodstains. Apply with a roller.

INTERIOR FILLER AND EMULSION PAINT

This mixture thickens the paint as opposed to diluting the colour, and is good for creating relief effects. Apply generously, using a paintbrush, or dip the stamp into the paint on a plate.

HOW TO APPLY PAINT

USING A ROLLER

Pour a little paint on to the side of a flat plate, then, using a sponge roller, pick up a small amount and roll it out over the rest of the plate until you have an even covering. Roll the paint on to the stamp.

USING A PAINTBRUSH

Use a fairly stiff brush and apply the paint with a dabbing or stippling motion. This technique enables more than one colour to be applied and for detail to be picked out. Be careful not to over-load the stamp, as this may cause it to slip when stamping.

DIPPING INTO PAINT ON A PLATE

Brush a thin coat of paint on to a flat plate, then press the stamp into the paint. You may need to do this several times to get an even coating. Initially the stamp will absorb a good amount of paint. Keep brushing more paint on to the plate.

USING A ROLLER AND BRUSH

Use a sponge roller to apply the paint evenly over the whole stamp. Use a brush to apply a second colour to act as a highlight or shadow, or to pick out details of the design.

USING A SPONGE

Spread the paint on a plate, then use a natural sponge to pick up the paint and dab it on to the stamp. This method allows you to put a light, even covering of paint on to the stamp.

USING AN INKSTAMP PAD

Press the stamp on to the inkpad several times to ensure a good covering. This technique will give a dry look to the stamp.

PREPARING SURFACES

TILES, CHINA AND GLASS
These are all prepared in the same way, using soapy water to remove dirt and grease, then drying with a lint-free cloth. Appropriate specialist paints must be used as normal emulsion (latex) and acrylic paints will not adhere well and are not sufficiently durable for these surfaces.

1 Wash the tile or glass with soapy water and rinse thoroughly. To remove any remaining traces of grease, give the surface a final wipe with a cloth dipped in methylated spirits and leave to dry.

2 When printing on a curved surface, carefully roll the stamp while holding the object securely. Sponge stamps are best suited for this purpose. Rubber stamps are less suitable.

FABRICS
Fabrics must be washed and ironed before stamping to remove any dressing and allow for any shrinkage. Again, use specialist fabric paint so that the item can be washed. Fix the paint according to the manufacturer's instructions.

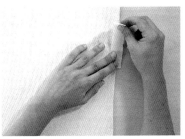

1 Once ironed, lay the fabric on a flat surface and tape the edges to hold it steady.

2 Place a piece of cardboard or scrap paper under the area to be stamped to stop any paint bleeding through the fabric.

WOOD
Wood should be lightly sanded before stamping and varnished afterwards. When using wood-stains, keep the stamp quite dry to stop the stain bleeding into the grain of the wood.

1 Sand the surface and wipe down with a soft cloth to remove any loose dust.

2 Once dry, the stamped design can be rubbed back to create a distressed effect.

PLANNING A DESIGN

1 With the aid of a spirit level (carpenter's level), draw a faint pencil line to use as a guide when stamping.

2 Stamp the motif several times on scrap paper and cut out the prints. Tape them to the wall so that you can judge how your design will look.

3 When using a stamp mounted on a block, you can draw a straight line on the back to help with positioning. Align the block with the pencil guideline on the wall.

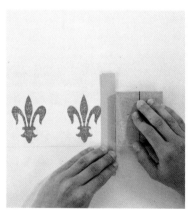

4 A piece of cardboard held between the previous print and the stamp will ensure consistent spacing between motifs.

5 For a tighter look, butt the stamped motifs together.

6 Once the paint is dry, the pencil guideline can be removed using a cloth wrung out in soapy water and rubbed along the line.

STAMP EFFECTS

You can achieve many different effects with stamps, depending on the paint mixture you use and the way it is applied. The same stamp, cut from high-density sponge, was used to make all these prints.

HALF-SHADE

Roll the first, paler colour over the stamp, then roll a second, darker shade over one half only, to create a three-dimensional shadowed effect.

TWO-TONE

Using a dry roller, load the stamp with the first colour, then apply the second to the top and bottom edges only.

TWO-TONE WITH DRY ROLLER

For an even subtler colour mix, roll the second colour right over the first using a very dry roller.

CONTRASTING DETAIL

Pick out details of the design in a contrasting colour: apply the first colour with a roller, then use a brush to apply the second colour in the areas you want.

PARTIAL OUTLINE

This shadow effect is produced by stamping the motif in one colour, then partially outlining the print using a paintbrush or felt-tip pen.

DROP SHADOW

Another, very subtle, effect of shadows and highlights is produced by printing the motif in the darker colour first. When this is dry, load the stamp with the paler colour and print over the first image, positioning the stamp slightly to one side.

▶

STIPPLED

This stippled effect gives the print lots of surface interest: apply the paint with a stiff brush and a dabbing, stippling motion.

WALLPAPER PASTE

Adding wallpaper paste to emulsion (latex) paint gives the print a translucent, watercolour quality.

LIGHT SHADOW

The paint has been applied with a roller, covering each element of the motif more heavily on one side to create a delicate shadow effect.

SECOND PRINT

After loading the stamp with paint, print first on a piece of scrap paper. This very delicate image is the second print.

SPONGE PRINT

Applying the paint with a sponge gives variable, individual prints.

DISTRESSED

A single colour applied with a dry roller produces an aged, distressed effect.

TEMPLATES

Enlarge the templates on a photocopier, or trace the design and draw a grid of evenly spaced squares over your tracing. Draw a larger grid on to another piece of paper and copy the outline square by square. Draw over the lines to make sure they are continuous.

Gothic Dining Room pp 54–57

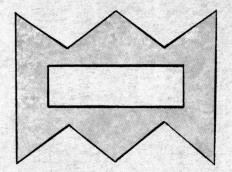

Sante Fe Living Room pp 36–39

Plaster Wall Treatment pp 50–53

Moorish Tile-effect pp 30–33

Folk-art Chair pp 40–42

Scandinavian Bedroom pp 64–67

Grape-vine Frieze and Glasses pp 12–15

Strawberry Trug pp 19–21

Art Nouveau Roses pp 46–49

Sailing-boat Frieze
pp 60–63

SUPPLIERS

The specialist materials and equipment that you will require for the stamping projects featured in this book are available from any good art supply shop.

Cornelissen & Son Ltd
105 Great Russell Street
London WC1B 3RY

Crown Paints
Crown Decorative Products Ltd
PO Box 37
Crown House
Hollins Road
Darwen
Lancashire BB3 0BG

Daler-Rowney Ltd
PO Box 10
Southern Industrial Estate
Bracknell
Berkshire RG12 8ST

London Graphic Centre
16 Shelton Street
London WC2H 9JJ
Specialist art supplies

Paint Magic
79 Shepperton Road
Islington
London N1 3DF

E. Ploton Ltd
273 Archway Road
London N6 5AA
Art and gilding materials

Russell & Chapple Ltd
23 Monmouth Street
London WC2H 9DE

Stuart Stephenson Ltd
68 Clerkenwell Road
London EC1M 5QA
Art and gilding materials

Winsor & Newton
Whitefriars Avenue
Wealdstone
Harrow
Middlesex HA3 5RH

ACKNOWLEDGEMENTS

The publishers would like to thank the following people for designing the projects in this book: Petra Boase for the Flower-pot Frieze pp 8–11, Animal Frieze pp 68–71, Starry Cabinet pp 72–4, Stamped Wrapping Paper pp 75–7, Regal Photo Album pp 78–9; Sacha Cohen for the Moorish Tile-effect pp 30–33, Santa Fe Living Room pp 36–9, Plaster Wall Treatment pp 50–53, Gothic Dining Room pp 54–7, Scandinavian Bedroom pp 64–7; Lucinda Ganderton for the Grape-vine Frieze and Glasses pp 12–15, Strawberry Trug pp 19–21, Folk-art Chair pp 40–42, Tartan Linen Box pp 43–5, Art Nouveau Roses pp 46–9, Sailing-boat Frieze pp 60–63; Liz Wagstaff for the Mexican-style Chopping Boards pp 16–18, Spotted Flower Pots pp 22–3, Herb Box pp 24–6, Sun-star Blind pp 27–9, Valentine Lampshade pp 34–5, Indian Velvet Cushion pp 58–9.

INDEX